Women and Time

By John G. Agno and Barbara A. McEwen

Copyright 2011

ISBN: 9780983586579

Table of Contents

Forward

Introduction

Expectations

Different Expectations

Why Gender Matters

Managing Stress

Anger: A Second Emotion

Meeting Expectations: Theirs and Yours

It's About Choices

It is Not Your Fault

Master the Skill of Focusing

Weary Women Don't Get the Life They Want

Feeling You 'Have To'

The Elephant in the Room

We Get What We Tolerate

Know Thyself

What is Your Life Signature?

Assumptions Drive Behavior

Your Personal Vision/Mission

Lack of Purpose = Lack of Focus

Will You Set Goals or Have Elusive Dreams?

Self-Sabotage

The Possibility of Having it All

The Pathway to Happiness

Become the Same Person at Work and Home

Changing Outdated Beliefs

Close the Value Gap

We Need to Negotiate What We Want

Do What You Do Best

Winning at Work

Know What is Important

Do What Gets You What You Desire

Establishing Priorities

Think: Pareto Principle (The 80/20 Rule)

Multitasking Pitfalls

<u>Delegating</u>

<u>Perils of Procrastination</u>

<u>Take Action</u>

<u>Getting Organized</u>

<u>Get in Alignment with Your To-Do List</u>

<u>Time Wasters</u>

<u>Schedule Think Times</u>

<u>Be Clear About Your Availability</u>

<u>Energy, Time and Performance</u>

<u>Your Attitude is Everything</u>

<u>After Thought</u>

<u>About the Authors</u>

Forward

The concept for this book came about because of the frustrations and conflict routinely expressed by female coaching clients; There is so much to do and so little time.

There have been many articles and books that focus on time management written by men who don't understand female biology or female socialization. Having read books by many male authors, it's clear that they have one or more women doing a considerable amount of work for them -- essentially "taking care" of them. Is it any wonder that the time management books that are out there don't work well in relieving the pressures working women routinely face?

In examining this time management dilemma it became apparent that what these women were experiencing were not typical issues. Rather, they were trying to be all things to all people and had neglected their own priorities in the process. For the majority of women there is an underlying problem.

The theme all these women appear to dance to is: *Just Because I Can, I Think I Should.*

Despite long days and a never-ending series of ways for her to improve, these women continue to seriously undermine their health, their family life, their careers and important relationships. Something needs to be done.

From the perspective of the time-strapped woman, it was decided to reduce the content into valuable insights and ways in which women can quickly put the new insights into practice. For a complete explanation of the insights within this book, you are encouraged to purchase, "**When Doing It All Won't Do: A Self–**

<u>**Coaching Guide for Career Women**</u>" by Barbara McEwen and John Agno

Both books are dedicated to all those hard working women who are willing to embrace liberating change.

Introduction

Everyone you meet these days is overworked and out of time.

We live in a busy, noisy, complex and exciting world: where almost no one has enough time to make and act on their personal choices. In this 24/7 global economy, too many of us are feeling overly rushed and impatient, becoming easily distracted and forgetful. Dr. Edward Hallowell, a Sudbury, MA psychiatrist, goes further by saying he believes many of us are suffering from environmentally induced attention deficit disorder (A.D.D.), brought on by technology and activity overload. Not surprisingly, he feels that working women are particularly susceptible to this syndrome.

Working effectively, by prioritizing, planning ahead and scheduling without creating a stressful mindset, can be grouped under the heading of time management.

Increasing technological advances tend to be the consequences of living where everybody is trying to do more in less time.

Yet, we must be able to maintain our focus and restore our energy as we bend, stretch and bounce around at work and in our personal life. We know that if we don't prioritize our life activities, we'll find ourselves spread so thin that we won't have time for those people and things that are important to us.

Today, we have more timesaving helpers and systems than ever before. So, why isn't there enough time to juggle all the things we must do in our day? We are supposed to be experiencing an enhanced quality of life, and then we go ahead adding to our stress levels by taking on more tasks than we have resources to handle. There's a tremendous need for new methods, systems and, above all, habits to keep us on track.

The time management insights and tips presented in this book are geared to help you de-stress, re-energize and channel your time better. However, the heavy lifting to re-engineer your daily rituals and develop time management habits that work better will be painful while rewarding. Clarifying your time management intentions and paying daily attention to them must happen before a positive and permanent behavioral change can occur. As one who helps people to live a better life by taking control of their behavior, the author knows that these meaningful and practical tips are only the beginning in allowing your perceptions to evolve....so you may get to where you want to be in life and at work.

Only when we become aware of something, are we able to make good choices as to the action we wish to take.

What operates in the background of our time management behavior is surfaced and discussed in this book to help you learn what you don't know about how you make choices and compromises. We all rely heavily on intuition to gauge the course of our actions and unconsciously engage our default behavior.

Intuition is fast, automatic, unreasoned thought and feelings that harvest our experience and guide our lives. However, we can be blind-sided by costly intuitive errors when our brain's quick pattern recognition leads us astray. Our unconscious, implicit and emotional attitudes may not agree with our analytical brain. Intuition is powerful, often wise, but sometimes perilous when we over feel and under think.

The shadow of intuition is the fear factor. We fear what we can't control. We fear threats we have read about or seen on TV. We fear new concepts that are unfamiliar to us. We fear being wrong if we step outside our familiar rituals. We allow these intuitive fears to hijack our rational mind.

The challenge is to be yourself but with more decision-making skills. What is needed will vary from day to day and context to context. It's up to you to develop and refine your intuition and sensors, find ways to discover and selectively reveal your flaws and empathize with what's important in order to remain steadfast in allocating your limited time and energy.

It's our hope that, by looking inside yourself and selectively applying these time management insights and tips, you'll be able to control your two-track mind through balancing your automatic intuitive brain with your deliberate, analytical brain.

Expectations

"I feel there is something unexplored about women that only a woman can explore." Georgia O'Keefe

Different Expectations

"Don't tell me how hard you work. Tell me how much you get done." James Ling

Incredibly, all the people in our life -- of which there are many -- have subtle expectations of us.

We know deep down that we simply cannot meet all these expectations and the more we try to, the more we become frustrated and angry by all the demands people place on us.

But remember, we also have expectations of ourselves and others. This is an important realization since our expectations come from the way we were raised and it has a gender component. There is a tendency for each of us to bond most strongly with the same sex parent. Boys certainly love their mothers but strongly resist being viewed a mamma's boy. Girls like to compete, hit home runs and are proud to be daddy's little girl but they are still expected to emulate their mother's role -- behave properly, love babies and be good in the kitchen. This is obviously an over-simplification but the reality is there are numerous subtle expectations.

Having said that, even though girls have been told they can be anything they want to be, as they enter the workplace, they soon discover they are in conflict. They can be a stellar performer but are still expected to conform to societal norms--- help plan functions, smooth over relationships, cooperate, know their place and complete tasks in a timely manner.

All the while, in the home, there is little regard given for her executive position. She is still expected to be a supportive wife, an exceptional mother, a good friend and an ideal daughter. What to do about all these expectations?

Putting it into Practice

It's impossible to be all things to all people. Decide what is important for you. This may fluctuate but be aware that you can choose.

Get your supports in place now! From help with the home, to childcare, to meal preparation, to gift buying, to all sorts of tasks we are expected to perform. Find the people you need whether you pay for services or get friends and relatives, or your partner to assist.

Learn to involve others. Learning to delegate, teach and train those around you to do what you expect of them. Take the time at work to develop your staff and build their capabilities. At home do the same thing. We teach people how to treat us. If you are constantly playing the female role of picking up after everyone – don't be surprised when they let you.

Why Gender Matters

"You don't have to act like a man to succeed in business for you will always be judged as a woman." Pat Heim

There has been an ongoing controversy about whether gender is even an issue we should be discussing as it relates to professional women and time management.

The truth is that men and women often approach a broad range of career issues differently. Consider how it is that we convey competence, face competition, put forward our ideas, get involved in corporate politics, or how we determine our role on a team. Many career-oriented women unwittingly make mistakes that undermine their credibility, simply because of gender expectations and misconceptions.

Forget the stereotyping that "boys are competitive, girls are collaborative."   In recent years scientists have discovered that differences between the sexes are more profound than anybody previously guessed.   Here is what Dr. Leonard Sax, MD, PhD says we now know for sure:

The female brain develops differently. In women, the language areas of the brain develop before the areas used for spatial relations and for geometry. In men, it's the other way around.

The female brain is wired differently. In women, emotion is processed in the same area of the brain that processes language. So, it's easy for most women to talk about their emotions. In men, the brain regions involved in talking are separate from the regions involved in feeling. The hardest question for many men to answer is: "Tell me how you feel."

Men and women respond to stress differently. Not just in our species, but in every mammal scientists have studied. Stress enhances learning in males. The same stress impairs learning in females. Interesting, isn't it.

Add hormones to the mix and you can readily see the importance of recognizing the differences between men and women, particularly when they are under stress or multi-tasking.

It is completely natural for women to respond differently in a wide variety of areas. Because our brains are wired differently, we are more emotional and more verbal. We not only want our position to be heard but at the same time we also want understanding.

Men shy away from the emotional because it does not come naturally to them. They are more pragmatic and quickly get into the "Mr. Fix It" mode. They'll hear you express a concern. Immediately, without much forethought or dialogue, they will want to fix it for you. They jump right into problem solving and then want you to get on with it.

As you can imagine, the gender gap can create all sorts of problems when neither side feels valued or understood. "I gave her the solution, why didn't she take it?" or "I just need to talk this through and he didn't hear a word I said." Sound familiar?

Putting it into Practice

Beware of gender gaps. Recognize that ingrained behaviors can create a "gender gap." Understand that within a personal relationship or communicating with your male coworkers, it will be up to you to identify ways to bridge this gender gap to improve the situation. Why? Because, in general, they don't know what they don't know! Once you recognize what you need and what the other needs and expects you can more readily navigate the terrain successfully.

Prefacing your comments, with "I'd just like you to hear me out" or "I just need your help in thinking this through" may help. Asking him to wait before offering solutions may also force him to listen to the entire message. Remember, once he gives you his advice, he likely will expect you to take it. You, on the other hand, may want to hear what he has to say but you might also seek out the advice of others before taking action. Gender differences are real. Women need to be consciously aware of some of the common pitfalls. Stressing over these types of situations is an unproductive use of your time. Better to be aware and work on solutions.

Be Self–Aware. Personality, in addition to our reactions is also gender–based. We react the way we have been trained to react from an early age. These reactions may or may not be working for you. Examining your stress or default behavior, along with your expectations will likely shed some light on what is important to you. Many women under stress simply will stop talking. Remember, how the brain has developed and is wired differently. It is language based. Men, on the other hand become strategic and tactical. Stress revs them up. It becomes a competition.

Take this familiar situation: Returning home after work you want to reduce the stress of the day. You'd like to get dinner over with and get things organized for the next day -- you're never done! Your partner may have a totally different way of reducing his stress. He sees his work day as done. He may want to unwind in front of the TV or read the paper. Both are valid. From the female perspective this is not fair. And, we know women always want things to be fair. Now is time to negotiate what both need in order to function optimally. Understanding your own needs and the needs of the other person is the key. To have a workable balance, either he is willing to help or outside sources will be required.

Practice stress reduction. Allow yourself to engage in stress reduction activities to manage your stress. Seemingly this is a simple thing. However, stress reduction takes practice. Your needs may be totally different from what others need. Find what works for you -- not just going through the motions because someone else enjoys it. Once you find it. Then do it.

Managing Stress

"Is everything as urgent as your stress would imply?" Carrie Latet

We live in stressful times. That is not an understatement. We are hearing about record home foreclosures, a fragile economy, and are watching the value of our investments decline. Things we have little control over.

Coupled with this, we are keenly aware of all the many things we are responsible for -- from managing the home, maintaining relationships, handling workplace issues, looking after our health, to name a few. Then there are all the expectations that others have of us, from spouses, to children, to relatives, to employers, to teachers and neighbors.

Although most of us recognize that moderate stress can help us to perform at a higher level, persistent stress can be debilitating and dangerous. Stress eats away at our ability to manage both our time and our responsibilities. Hopefully, you are not one of those who want to wear their stress as a badge of honor to show how much you can handle! Beware: Stress has a major impact both physically and psychologically. When we are continually under chronic stress, our body reacts whether we are aware of it or not.

Each of us has a limit beyond which stress becomes toxic, even deadly. Our resistance is lowered, our performance declines, our mental well being gets derailed. There isn't a quick fix but successful people learn how to manage their stress.

Putting it into Practice

Manage your life, manage your stress. Routinely create some healthy distance from your difficulties and the expectations of others. Participate in activities that give you pleasure. Nurture friendships with those people who make you feel good about yourself. Try laughing more. You could also start a Gratitude Journal. Each day for at least a month write down three new things you are grateful for.

Take another perspective. Look at the stressful situation from various perspectives rather than just your own. Get input from others. Explore all the possibilities. Be determined to take action and embrace the change.

We're not talking churchology or religiousity. Whatever your belief system, it is important to believe in something greater than yourself. For some, this spiritual journey will be through their religious pursuits. For others it will be a commitment to practices that illuminates their life purpose or life signature. Then there are those who will simply want to acknowledge that life is a gift and to recognize the importance of taking care of your body with exercise, extra sleep and healthy food. We recommend you commit to the type of spiritual practice that helps fuel the light that is within.

Anger: A Second Emotion

"There are two primary choices in life; to accept conditions as they exist, or accept the responsibility for changing them."
Denis Waitley

Whether all these expectations make us angry with ourselves or with someone else, it is helpful to recognize that anger is a second emotion.

Anger can surface as a result of feeling overwhelmed by our roles or by being hurt, mistreated, or misunderstood. Anger, stems from the messages we tell ourselves that gets us all worked up. This can result from having unmet expectations of another, misplaced assumptions or even inaccurate information. Swallowing your anger or lashing out is not productive. Since anger is a valid emotion that wastes an excessive amount of time, we all need to make our anger works for us. When someone or something has violated our boundaries or offended us in some way, we need to protect ourselves accordingly.

Putting it into Practice

Anger is a valid emotion. Since anger is a secondary emotion, pay attention to getting in touch with the primary emotion. Do you have an unrealistic expectation of another? Have you been disappointed? Have you experienced a lack of respect? Has someone not trusted you? It is important to name it, in order to tame it.

We choose our behavior. Nobody actually "makes" you angry. We all have the power to choose how we will respond to any given situation. Decide how you want to respond to achieve the desired outcome.

We are all storytellers. As mentioned earlier, in addition to brain development, women have been socialized to be relaters and as such one of the first things women will do when angered is to stop talking. Internally, we begin to expand on the stories we tell ourselves about our predicament. Then we search for information to support the stories we tell our self. Be careful, because the story grows, often in disproportion to the actual event. Rather, try using a more assertive approach. Address the concerns while still being respectful of yourself and others. Use 20/20 hindsight. After the event is over, think about how you handled the situation. Look for the mistakes that were in the story you told yourself, so you don't continue to fall into the same trap. Identify what worked and what you could do differently the next time.

Let it go. Forgiveness, although not easy, releases us from the grip of another person or the situation that originally angered us. Focusing on the wrongdoing merely burdens us, wastes valuable time, and stops us from living more fully.

Meeting Expectations: Yours and Theirs

"Whatever your age, your upbringing, or your education, what you are made of is mostly unused potential." George Leonard

We all tell ourselves stories and then look for evidence that these stories and our interpretation of them are true. One of the stories women tend to tell themselves is "I am perfectly capable of doing it myself, so why wouldn't I?"

We don't want to admit that we are having a difficult time keeping up with all of these expectations. It makes us uncomfortable to think we are incapable of handling everything that life throws at us. We are very aware of what others expect and they expect a lot. It is one of the reasons we don't trade getting help for less stressful living. Instead, we take on a "can do" attitude to build up our own ego.

When we do this, we are really being shortsighted. What we are really saying is, "I would rather have a stressful marriage and risk divorce than spend a few dollars and prove I can do it all." Or, "I would rather be stressed out and yell at my kids than give someone some of my money." Or, "It is not worth the fight, I don't see any options." There are always options and there are always choices.

Putting it into Practice

Identify the stressors in your life. Of all of the stressors, what is the ONE THING that you could do that would give you the most benefit? Be honest with yourself. Now identify why it is that you are not doing what would be most helpful. If it is money, then let's look at that. If it is something else, then lets deal with that.

When you name it, you can tame it. If it is money, then identify where you can save if you eliminated the non essentials. Take- out food, too many extra-curricular activities for the children, impulsive spending, to name a few. There are always ways where you can save money to get the support you need. A more content you, is a more content family. As the old saying goes "When momma's not happy, nobody is happy." Isn't change worth it?

Choose not to carry the pain. Is it something else? Identify what is the pain you are associating with not taking action. By doing this, you will understand what is holding you back. Is the pain of dealing with these issues greater than doing it all yourself? Remember, what we tolerate grows - the frustration will grow worse over time. Can you afford not to deal with what is causing pain?

See the benefits. Now write out the benefits you'll receive if you put a simple plan in place to change the ONE THING that gives you the most stress. Believe me, you'll begin to feel in control of your life, your energy will surge, and your self-confidence will return. Today is the time to begin.

It's About Choices

"Destiny is no matter of chance. It is a matter of choice: It is not a thing to be waited for, it is a thing to be achieved." William Jennings Bryan

It is Not Your Fault

"One thing you can't recycle is wasted time." Author Unknown

Traditional time management and organizing techniques are designed for linear thinkers who organize by timelines, calendars, to-do lists, processing one thing at a time.

More creative people have minds that feel like they are running in many different directions at once. People who are visual or kinesthetic can also have problems with traditional time management techniques. Customary time management techniques don't take each of our unique personalities into account. Don't feel guilty. Instead, recognize the way your personality, your mind and your body work. Learn and develop techniques that work for you – not someone else.

Putting it into Practice

Gain insight into yourself. And other key people in your life. This cannot be underestimated. Knowing who you are and identifying key strengths and abilities will be helpful. Getting clear on what you are meant to do will give you the energy and passion to transform your life. Understand your capabilities and where support or systems are necessary.

It is a myth that business rewards the smart. Once you get to a certain level in business everyone is smart. They all have the technical competencies necessary to fulfill the role they were hired to do. If that is the case, who is more likely to accelerate their success? Studies reveal in business: The skills that initially got you in the door are not the same skills required to progress.

First and foremost, after a certain level, business rewards social and emotional competencies. Don't lose sight of this important lesson. Stop yourself if you are inclined to get so busy completing tasks that you ignore developing your contacts and network of influential key players. For women, it is also essential that they remember the importance of keeping your emotions under control.

You're unique. Daily you are building your brand. Whether you recognize it or not; the good, the bad and the ugly. Tune into how others are seeing you. It is your responsibility to develop your strengths and create a personal persona that you are happy with. It is also up to you to identify how you want to approach your work and your personal life. Following these lessons will give you the power to use your talent most effectively.

Master the Skill of Focusing

"It is not who you think you are that holds you back but what you think you're not." Author Unknown

Why am I so easily distracted? At the end of the day, I haven't completed anywhere near what I had planned to do. I write lists but the lists just seem to get longer and longer. What is one to do?

A disciplined mind is a wonderful thing. All peak performers have disciplined themselves to clear their mind of mental chatter so they are able to concentrate on important tasks. One of the most beneficial qualities a person can develop is the ability to focus for an extended period of time. In the *Top 200 Secrets to Success and Pillars of Self-Mastery*, Robin S. Sharmon tells us some techniques for learning to build up your concentration muscles. Follow these simple exercises and no large task will again haunt you.

Putting it into Practice

The Two Minute Mind. Simply stare at the second hand on your watch for two minutes and think about nothing else for that time. At first the mind will wander but after 21 days of practice, your attention will not waver during the routine.

The power of focus. To enhance your concentration and the power of focus, count your steps when you walk. Take six steps while taking a long inhale, hold your breath for another six steps, and then exhale for six steps. If six steps are too long, do what feels comfortable. You will feel alert, refreshed, and internally quiet and centered after this exercise. Recognize and appreciate the power of a quiet mind.

Create new habits. Get into the habit of memorizing; either beautiful poetry or a passage or quote from a favorite book. Practice for only 5 minutes a day and enjoy the results of developing the ability to focus for extended periods of time.

Weary Women Don't Get the Life They Want

"The Statue of Liberty is no longer saying, 'Give me your poor, your tired, your huddled masses.' She's got a baseball bat and yelling, 'You want a piece of me?'" Robin Williams

Instead of having the freedom to enjoy life, women get weary from all the chores they think they have to do.

Do you recognize the weary and the whiny? Do you recognize that often weary women will wield their tongue like whips? During times when it is most important time for us to be well balanced and wise, we lash out or become aggressive, sullen or unreachable. Then we think about our kids. They are growing up too fast. What kind of an example are we setting? We know we can't turn back the clock and regain lost time. This is not what we intended.

Isn't it time that we recognize that we are doing too much, we're too busy and too tired. As Dr. Phil would say, "How's this working for you?" If it isn't, then it is time to focus on what is important to you. Never let the things that matter most be taken over by things that matter least.

Putting it into Practice

Life is not a dress rehearsal. Life is the real performance and you need to allow yourself to enjoy the journey. Set aside time each morning to plan your day. Plan around your priorities and focus only on those tasks that are important to you.

Shut the door on "Superwoman." Open the door to the life you want. Several times throughout the day, ask yourself if what you are doing is the best use of your time and energy.

Stop blaming yourself. When you fail to get everything done there is always another day. Things are never so urgent that you need to put yourself under all that pressure. Say goodbye to stress by not thinking that every problem you encounter is your responsibility. Remember, choose what is important and what needs your attention. Decide what it is that others can do, for you and themselves and for others.

Feeling You "Have To'"

"In truth, people can generally make time for what they choose to do; it is not really the time but the will that is lacking." Sir John Lubbock

Women have been conditioned to feel "they have to." Since we were young we've been taught to believe that hard work, determination and looking after others will get us what we want -- even if we are not the nurturing kind.

I can't tell you how many times, as a coach, I hear how female clients allow others to set expectations for them. Direct reports continue to manage up. All the employee has to say is, "I can't do this, or I haven't the time" and the female manager will begrudgingly take on the job. They do it because they're used to picking up whether it is for family or direct reports. They are acting motherly or womanly... falling into a cleanup role, often to their disadvantage.

And they're resentful and frustrated because they thought this made them successful. Unfortunately, it is just this type of behavior that has stifled their career. They are viewed as being taken advantage of and seen as ineffective in developing their team, nor are they embracing the power of their position. This behavior sends the subtle message -- women are busy taking care while men are busy taking charge.

Putting it into Practice

Hard work doesn't guarantee the results you want. Remind yourself that the willing horse gets the heavy load but not necessarily the promotion. You are accountable to your boss to see that tasks come in on time and on budget.

However, it is also your role to ensure that staff are fully trained, given the right supports and undertake full responsibility for their assigned duties.

Wish you had a wife? Most working women quickly acknowledge that they wish they did. You have two choices- you can stop thinking about all the chores that need doing before you can relax, or you can choose to get the right supports in place to help you manage the tasks that need doing.

Manage the home. In most households, the house work is not evenly divided. Don't allow this to drive you into a martyr role that will adversely affect your family relationships. If you view yourself as a good manager, don't ignore your manager's role in the home.

The Elephant in the Room

"Until we can manage time, we can manage nothing else." Peter F. Drucker

The common cliché "the elephant in the room" simply means a problem that everyone is well aware of but the group has set up a conspiracy of silence because nobody is willing to deal with the issue. Putting "one's head in the sand" is supposedly in place to protect those involved from taking action. This lack of action, whether out of fear, conflict avoidance or embarrassment, only aggravates the problem because everyone knows what is going on and the situation is impossible to ignore.

Beliefs such as "Some things are better left unsaid," "It's not my problem," or "I'm not going to rock the boat" only allow the deception to continue. Effective women do not allow these conditions to continue.

Putting it into Practice

Ignoring the problem won't help. The issue must be addressed in a non-threatening atmosphere. Focus on the facts and the behavior, not on personality. Avoid blame or labeling the behavior. Stay away from using words such as always, never, or why. They put the hearer on the defensive.

The art of the question. Use probing or clarifying questions when addressing the issue. This helps the individual view their actions from the vantage point of others. Encourage an honest evaluation of performance linking past actions to future improvements.

Be supportive. Use a conversational tone rather than allowing yourself to sound upset. Focus on the future rather than the past. Get a commitment on what specific actions will be taken within an agreed upon time-line. Follow-up.

We Get What We Tolerate

"Any goal that forces you to labor, day after day and year after year, so long and hard that you never have any time for yourself and those you love is not a goal but a sentence ... a sentence to a lifetime of misery, no matter how much wealth and success you attain." Og Mandino

Are you surprised that you are getting what you tolerate?

In medicine, we look at how well a drug can be tolerated in respect to its side effects. At work and at home, many people evaluate their duties the same way --- how well certain aspects can be tolerated.

Often there can be a temptation to ignore some of the more upsetting aspects of life and work with the idea that we just don't need the aggravation of challenging the status quo. Seeking painless solutions to life's tensions, repeating your own behavior that hasn't worked in the past, or taking the safe route for fear of a negative response is just not realistic.

Reflect on it. If you have been tolerating a certain behavior to avoid conflict, it is very likely that what you have been tolerating has grown. Just as energy is wasted by fretting about things that are not important, you waste valuable time by not addressing things that need to be addressed. We are not saying you need to become overzealous in addressing every single little thing that bothers you. Nor, are we saying you need to be the bad cop or the intolerant parent. To paraphrase Aristotle, seek to address the issues that are important to you, doing so at the right time, for the right reason and in the right way.

Putting it into Practice

Confront issues early. Stay on top of problems and don't let them escalate.

Have a Plan. Don't respond out of anger. Structure how you will raise the issue, name the troubling behavior and discuss the implication. Deal with the individual in a positive manner. View them as a work in progress.

Listen to Learn. Ask what steps the person will take to address the issue now that it has been identified. To have the person respond favorably it will be important to stop talking and start listening. If you don't listen to them, it is unlikely they will listen to you. Schedule time to regularly give feedback, it will reduce the anxiety that often surfaces when issues need to be addressed.

Know Thyself

"Before one can truly manage time, it is important to know where you are going, what your priorities and goals are, and in which direction you are headed. Where you are headed is more important than how fast you are going. Rather than always focusing on what's urgent, learn to focus on what is really important." Oprah Winfrey

What is your Life Signature?

"No man is born into the world whose work is not born with him." James Russell Lowell

We are all spiritually driven. But that energy can be dissipated if our actions are scattered and we feel pulled in a various directions. Once we know who we are and what we're meant to do, we have new-found energy that pulls us forward. When we don't know, we feel we are spinning our wheels; we're tired and not accomplishing much.

Our life signature is the tracing of the talents we are given and how we express them in our lives.

Defining our life signature begins by tracing our talents back over the years. There are a growing percentage of people thinking about the meaning of their life. This genuine spiritual concern is broader than traditional views of religion practiced in numerous countries of the world. Yet, it is unclear to most how to live their life in a meaningful way.

Putting it into Practice

Change takes practice. It is very hard to bring about significant change without changes in behavior. Powerful countervailing forces appear when we attempt to engineer positive change alone. Although you can do it on your own, a coach or mentor will help to more quickly navigate the hunt toward discovering your life signature. You will be required to make a commitment to staying focused and being prepared.

Let your life signature be your guide. Once discovered, you will know where and how to leverage your time.

Know what is important. Spending time on what's important adjusts your focus toward potentially positive outcomes, instead of negative ones.   By knowing who you are and what you are meant to do, you don't waste time tolerating what's not important. This results in <u>building your innate signature talents</u> into well developed strengths while experiencing a sense of well–being and <u>increased self–awareness</u>.

Assumptions Drive Your Behavior

"It's not hard to make decisions when you know what your values are." Roy Disney

We say that time management is a symptom because there is an underlying problem. Not paying attention to your intentions is the problem. Articulating our implicit assumptions is critical to becoming aware of why we do what we do. Becoming conscious of our "default thinking" helps us to be aware of our inherited purpose. Looking back in our life to those life–defining moments gives us plenty of clues on how to discover our <u>life purpose</u> or <u>life signature</u>.

Putting it into Practice

Being clear on your intangible assumptions allows you to engineer a dynamic equilibrium... where all the parts of your life work synergistically in a highly interrelated whole. Here are the intangibles that form the foundation of a strategic time management action plan:

We all make assumptions and hold strong beliefs. Recognize that these assumptions and beliefs are continuously reinforced through our experiences. These are the mental models we use to create our work and personal lives.

Our Values and Guiding Principles depict our world-view. These values and principles are easily observed by others through one's behavior. Values often influence people's choices about where to invest their energies. Please recognize that values change over time. Being "fair" means something different for a person at 54 than someone at 14. A guiding principle is a universal operating standard that guides decision-making both personally and organizationally.

Create a PersonalVision. A personal vision or mission becomes our own mental picture of how we see our future unfolding. We energize people to support our purpose or life signature with an overarching description of what we see.

Your Personal Vision/Mission

"Our deeds determine us, as much as we determine our deeds."
George Elliot

Much of our problem with time management is that we have not given enough thought to who we are and what makes us unique. We highly recommend you consider developing a personal mission statement.

A mission statement is simply a set of guiding principles which clearly state how you are going to live your life and for what purpose. It is short, it embodies your personal values and like a GPS it keeps you going in the right direction.

If each of us is on this earth for a reason, then it holds true that there is a unique purpose for each one of us. Life is about finding that reason for being and then living that reason out. We've all seen some sad lives. They are the lives of woulda, coulda, shoulda. Looking at these lives, you see a person who feels that they never really found their purpose. Somehow throughout life they just missed it. On the other hand, we all know of people whose lives are on fire... they easily inspire us.

We encourage you to take the time to be introspective. Look back and identify the golden threads that run through your life. Discover your uniqueness through dialogue and appreciative inquiry, either with a family member, friend, spiritual group or coach.

Putting it into Practice

Name what is important. Before getting started, write out those things that are most important to you. Keep them foremost in your mind as you proceed.

Create a mission statement. Begin by writing down as many guiding principles as you can. Principles are the types of things that you want to govern your life. Here are a few examples: If I take on a job, it is worth doing well; I'll associate only with positive and inspiring people; I'll be respectful and polite but never be pushed around; I'll stay fit -- strong people are mentally tough. You get the idea...

We set the stage for our life. It is our belief that we are expected to be co-creators in our own life's story - to follow our own dreams, to believe in our self, and to make a difference. Whether you are 17 or 70, we recommend you to take time to uncover your life's mission. Here's a clue: your signature strengths and your dreams go hand-in-hand. We owe it to ourselves, to go after our dreams and find our reason for being.

Staying on your chosen path. You may want a mission/purpose statement but you will actually have to take the time to dialogue about it, write it down and memorize it. Whatever you come up with, you will need to take the time to refine it as much as possible. A good mission statement is less than 25 words -- something you can easily remember. Then when something unexpected happens, or you are pulled off course, you can simply go back to your mission statement and return to your chosen path.

Lack of Purpose = Lack of Focus

"Money will come to you when you are doing the right things for the right reason." Michael Phillips

More on your mission/purpose statement....

We are born with a job to do and have been given the talent, virtues and circumstances needed to fulfill that role.

Our task is to uncover exactly what is our unique purpose or mission. Part of the process is uncovering our strengths and then consciously building upon these competencies.

Once we identify our life's mission, we then become co-creators in our own life's journey. All kinds of wonderful and exciting things happen. We connect with people of like-mind. Opportunities surface. We are clear on our direction. Time becomes our friend.

Putting it into Practice

There are golden threads that run through your life. You've already detailed the principles you want to live by. That is good. The next step is to write out the specific areas in your life where you have had personal success.

Values are tightly held beliefs. We act on our values by choice and they are important to us. They are the types of things that people will know you by. Here are some examples:

Honest, trustworthy, eager, competent, flexible, approachable, etc. Write out your values.

Giving back. Consider how it is you would like to contribute to society as a whole. Write these out.

Will You Set Goals or Have Elusive Dreams?

"You are the embodiment of the information you choose to accept and act upon. To change your circumstances you need to change your thinking and subsequent actions." Adlin Sinclair

Now that you have developed a solid sense of self, it is time to establish your personal goals. These will link directly to your personal mission statement.

Setting goals is about taking action. Otherwise your vision of the future will remain just an elusive dream. It is a powerful process designed to help you choose what you want to do to turn your vision into a reality. It involves documenting your decisions and disciplining yourself. The intent is to help you establish clearly defined goals that can be measured and quantified.

First, envision the overview of what it is you want to achieve in your life. Once you can see the big picture, it will be easy to break these down into smaller and smaller initiatives. Think in terms of goals that are in the following intervals -- 1 to 2 years, 3 to 5 years and 5 to 10 years. Your goals should be constantly evolving. As you achieve your goals, record your successes and modify your plan. Celebrate your achievements.

Good goals include these categories: Physical; Professional; Financial; Family/Relationships; Communication, Personal Development; Location/Residence; Hobbies; and Service

Putting it into Practice

Establish your goals. Under the three time intervals above, write out each of your goals. Keep them precise, achievable and incremental.

Prioritize each one and assign target dates. Plan to do the most important first – not the easiest. Setting time lines will keep you moving forward.

Track your achievements and celebrate your success. As you make goal setting part of your life, you'll find increased enthusiasm for updating and revising.

Self-Sabotage

"Until you value yourself, you will not value your time. Until you value your time, you will not do anything with it." M. Scott Peck

Looking from the outside, it is easy to see how some people have entrenched beliefs about how the world should work.

Problems occur when these beliefs don't align with our reality. The question we might want to ask is, "Why do we allow our decisions and behaviors to be influenced by these unrealistic beliefs?"

We've all received potentially destructive messages that go against what is true for us. Examples might include, "a certain task, is a woman's responsibility; or, stay-at-home women are better wives and mothers, than working women; or a good daughter looks after the emotional needs of their extended families. We self-sabotage when we don't address what are unrealistic beliefs for us. Often it is out of fear.

Fear definitely has a dark side. It distorts our thoughts. We want to avoid confrontation. Feeling powerless to change a challenging situation sends us into a downward spiral. We doubt ourselves and we doubt others. We stay stuck in emotionally charged situations.

Self-sabotage happens when you deny your responsibility for your life. You might ignore your own self-limits because you are trying to take care of other people whose love you desire. People begin to expect more from you than you physically or mentally are prepared to provide.

Putting it into Practice

We cannot control others. But we can control how we respond to another's expectation of us. Ideally, as we mature, we learn to successfully set limits and define our personal boundaries. In any given day, many people will make demands on our time, our talents, our energy, our money and emotions. It is up to us to choose what it is we will say 'no' to and what we will say 'yes' to. Every choice creates an outcome. This is also very much tied to our mission statement, so don't put that off.

Respect your own talent, power and potential. Harness your creative side. Put your skills to work by managing your resources and making them work for you. Identify the issues in your home/work life. Explore your options and look for solutions. No solution is ever achieved without taking action. Waiting for it to "work out" on its own will not resolve the issue.

Don't waste valuable time. Avoid seeing yourself as trapped in a situation or a victim of someone else's actions. Take full advantage of your ability to choose. See yourself as someone who is independent, capable and worthy.

The Possibility of Having It All

"But what is happiness except the simple harmony between a person and life they lead." Albert Camus

The Pathway to Happiness

"Happiness is produced not so much by great pieces of good fortune that seldom happen as by the little advantages that occur every day." Benjamin Franklin

"I will be happy when...." are the way many people go about living their lives. Happiness is being aware, not only of the positive events that occur in your life but, that we have choices in how we respond to unfortunate occurrences such as illness or accidents.

Putting it into Practice

Happiness isn't off in the future. It is living in the "now" and loving the moments of our daily experiences. We form an impression in every business or personal interaction. In the business world, we don't speak much about the heart. Yet, the purpose of doing our life's work should come from the heart- --since all businesses are ultimately people serving people. We all need connection, belonging and meaningful contribution.

Happiness isn't something that happens to you. Happiness is inside you now. We are all motivated from within. You only have to allow happiness to surface. You can use the power of your thoughts to focus on potentially positive outcomes, instead of potentially negative ones, and change your life.

Math matters when it comes to happiness.

$H = K \times D \times L$

The **H**appiness Formula = **K** (knowing who you are) multiplied by **D** (discovering your life's work) multiplied by **L** (learning not to tolerate what's not important).

Become the Same Person at Work and Home

"You can't move people to action unless you first move them with emotion. The heart comes before the head." John Maxwell

The roles you play at home and work must be in harmony... not requiring you to play different roles. Although there are distinct competencies attached to each role, it is to your advantage to create a powerful personal synergy among all your roles.

Creating a more holistic paradigm of integration with your work and home life will help you from thinking you are running between very different life segments. When you reach this new dynamic equilibrium, where all the parts of your life work synergistically in a highly interrelated whole, life balance happens. This synergy saves you incredible problem-solving time and energy.

Our overbooked lives and strong immunity to change try to keep us from relearning deeply in- grained habits. To make our intention a reality takes personal determination, practice, repetition and the support of others. Today, 64% of people in the U.S. say there is not enough time in the day to get things done.   A poor night's sleep and tight work deadlines adversely affect our performance.   We turn on the TV to pass the time rather then moving forward with focused action to accomplish our good intentions.

Putting it into Practice

Pay attention to your intentions. Every year, we gain a clearer understanding that without positive change, decline is inevitable. The challenge is to recognize that what we are now tolerating can be reinvented by paying attention to our intentions.

From where you are to where you want to be. Self-directed learning helps you to discover an ideal vision of yourself, to feel motivated in developing the abilities necessary to get you where you want to be. That is, you see the person you want to be---living with the capability necessary to create and sustain the new you. This becomes the source of the energy required to work at the difficult and often frustrating process of change.

It's tough to do it alone. Find the support to help you get to where you want to be. Others help us see things we are missing, affirm whatever progress we have made, test our perceptions and let us know how we are doing. They provide the context for our practice of the new rituals. Although the model is called self-directed learning, without others' involvement lasting change can't occur.

Changing Outdated Beliefs

"The law of sacrifice says you have to give up to go up." John Maxwell

It is possible for women to have it all, as long as we first change an outdated belief system that we need to do it all.

Putting it into Practice

Accept personal responsibility for your own life. This helps you transcend the stereotypical 'either/or judgmental thinking' of others, i.e. if you are a working woman you can't also be a good wife and mother.

Creating a balance. A certain amount of introspection and dialogue are necessary to learn what would be helpful for you to create integration between your world of work and your personal life. It takes some focused self-learning. Get to know yourself on an intimate level.

"Manage" the home. Consider managing your home life with the same efficiency that you manage the office. We don't, or shouldn't be, doing everything ourselves in our place of employment. It is expected that we will rely on others who have skills to do the jobs that simply aren't part of our role. The same is necessary in the home if a business woman wants to decrease her stress and have a well-balanced life.

Close the Value Gap

"We stand at the crossroad, each minute, each hour, each day, making choices. We choose the thoughts we allow ourselves to think, the passions we allow ourselves to feel, and the actions we allow ourselves to perform. Each choice is made in the context of whatever value system we've selected to govern our lives. In selecting that value system, we are, in a very real way, making the most important choice we will ever make." Benjamin Franklin

By definition, values are the ideals that guide our personal conduct. Values help us distinguish what is right from wrong. These values define us as individuals and it is how others view or judge our behavior.

Often there is a disconnect between the values we profess and how we actually behave. Integrity requires the alignment of our values – those core beliefs and behaviors that we have claimed are important to us. As a leader, our values must match our actions. So, if you say you value honest and open communications, but haven't been completely truthful lately, then by your own definition, your behavior is out of alignment. Most of us don't go around consciously violating our values, nor do we spend our days checking up on ourselves. However, when our behaviors contradict our values, not only do our bodies know it, but those we associate with will judge us harshly.

Putting it into Practice

Values open the door to our full potential. Since our values change over time it will likely be helpful every so often to re-write the values we aspire to.

Challenge the values that no longer fit. It is a good thing to throw out your old values – the ones that are not working well for you and needlessly work against you. Often there are values that have been passed down through the generations that simply don't match our belief systems. If they are unnecessary baggage you can choose to toss them away. Conversely, if we push down values that are important but not acted upon, they may need to be re-embraced.

Being authentic. Understanding your values will help steer you towards a life with meaning, clarity and authenticity. It helps us know what we should be concentrating on when the inevitable crisis in life bounces us around.

We Need to Negotiate What We Want

"Time = life; therefore, waste your time and waste of your life, or master your time and master your life." Author Unknown

Many males, both as spouses and business people, continue to view themselves as having authority, knowing all the answers, and being able to objectively look at a situation. Females, both as wives and working women, tend to focus on collaboration, valuing long-term interactions, and will tend to want to avoid confrontation. If you see yourself here, one of the key competencies you will need to develop is your negotiating skills.

Successful negotiations are a result of being prepared and knowing what you want to achieve. Be prepared to compromise, but neither side should feel they have surrendered to the demands of another. In addition to the work environment, negotiating at home with your partner and children will be necessary for all women. In both environments – work and home – you will be expected to be able to hold your ground, put forth your ideas succinctly without long rambling explanations, or undue emotions, and make a rational rather than emotional appeal for cooperation and future betterment of the situation.

Putting it into Practice

Connect. You will need to be able to connect (have mutual interests) with those you are negotiating with on specifically what is important to you.

Clarify. Describe with in-depth clarity why this is important to you.

Commit. Agree on a commitment to action that will be mutually beneficial to all concerned.

Do What You Do Best

"Nature arms each man with some faculty which enables him to do easily some feat impossible to any other." Ralph Waldo Emerson

Most of us try to live our lives with far too little information about how life really works.

If you think about it, everything in life... from kitchen gadgets to the tools we use, come with very detailed instructions. Pages of them. But the thing that matters most to us, life itself, comes with no instructions. We have to discover it ourselves!

Our personalities are shaped by genetics and life experiences. In childhood, we decide what's important to us and that influences a great deal of our personality. And, we continuously evolve. Each of us is defined by many things – our emotional habits, our belief systems, our pattern of thoughts, our cultural upbringing, our preferences, our motivations, our style of relating to others, to name a few.

Some characteristics we share in common, some we don't. What we need to function well will often be quite different from what someone else will need. This is where self-knowledge and personal insight comes in. There is a big advantage in knowing ourselves and the type of environment in which we feel nurtured. But there is also a huge advantage in knowing how a partner, a child, or a co-worker thinks, feels and sorts information. Once we recognize that not everyone is like me and that each of us sees the world through their own lens, we will quickly realize that individuals will approach similar situations differently. It is not necessary that they do it just like me.

Putting it into Practice

Self-understanding. You cannot afford to miss the richness that comes with understanding your own personality and the benefit it brings to relationships. Take time to explore one or two personality assessments, with or without a coach.

Learn your Signature Strengths. It has been said that foresight is better than hindsight but we believe insight tops them all. Learn your top five signature talents and understand how when they are overused can become a weakness. Understand how you stand out from others.

Self-Assessment Resources. As the world moves faster, when you are expected to do more with less, when teamwork and innovation are essential, when there are greater cultural and international concerns, understanding psychological types offers an unmatched resource.

www.SelfAssessmentCenter.com

Winning at Work

"Losers live in the past. Winners learn from the past and enjoy working in the present toward the future." Denis Waitley

Know What's Important and What's Not

"Things which matter most must never be at the mercy of things which matter least." Goethe

We promise ourselves that next time we'll just work a little harder or do it a little better. We can't cut anything out because, "It's all important!" We'll just get up a little earlier or go to bed a little later.

When we inevitably fail, we blame ourselves because, unlike Superwoman, we can't run faster than a speeding bullet, aren't more powerful than a locomotive, and don't leap tall buildings in a single bound. And our stress levels rise. It impacts us and it impacts those around us.

The truth is we're trying to do too much. And any juggler can only juggle so many balls in the air before they all come crashing down. When we don't learn the lessons, our problems just change clothes and march back into our lives.

Putting it into Practice

Not Everything is Important. When we say that everything is important it becomes impossible to prioritize. This irrational belief scatters our attention and defuses our focus. Allow yourself to recognize that not everything is important and know that only Superwoman can juggle it all.

Work Smarter, Not Harder. Say to yourself, "Working harder doesn't work for me. I need to do it smarter. I need to choose what is important and make good solid managerial choices."

Leadership is all about getting things done through others. People are anxious to follow those who have a vision. Use your leadership skills to get others to do the things that you need done. These will be things that can be easily delegated to others or, yes, you may need to pay to have them done.

Do What Gets You What You Want

"Everyone is self-made, only successful people are willing to admit it." Tom Bissmeyer

Believe it or not organizations seldom reward and promote the hardest workers.

Research shows that the hardest workers spend all their time working hard instead of working smart. The person who gets promoted is the one that understands the corporate direction, aligns their duties to the overarching goals, develops advantageous relationships and has a polished reputation.

Putting it into Practice

Be strategic. Be observant. Listen carefully and ask questions to uncover what it is that the company is looking for in its leaders. Follow the lead of star players.

Work for the sake of work doesn't work. The company needs growth and bottom line results. Look for what is actually rewarded, promoted and recognized. Don't be afraid to ask someone to mentor you, either inside or outside the organization. Look in areas where you may be weak – finance, marketing, sales or operations.

Start spending time on the things that matter. Stop doing the things you are doing that really don't matter. Think in terms of your boss's boss. View your job and position through his or her eyes and start doing what really counts. Time management is about focusing on what is important by preserving and enhancing relationships that achieve results.

Establishing Priorities

"It's not enough to be busy, so are the ants. The question is: What are we busy about?" Henry David Thoreau

To paraphrase Stephen R. Covey, in his book the *7 Habits of Highly Effective People*, "Effective management is really about putting the most important things first and getting the desired outcome. Effective leadership, on the other hand, is about the ability to determine what is important and for what reason."

Your task will be to do both. There is an old saying, "When everything is important, nothing becomes important." It is necessary for each of us to determine what is important to us. Nobody at the end of their days wishes they had worked more. Our life goals need to be in sync with our daily goals so we keep what is important first and foremost in our minds.

Putting it into Practice

Determine what is important in your life. Examine your personal strengths and resolve to discover what gives you a sense of purpose. There are all kinds of resources available to you.

Connect your priorities to what is important in your life. Gaining this type of clarity will impact the decisions you make, the goals you establish and where you choose to spend your time.

Learn to say 'No.' It is only when you have a clear sense of your personal purpose that you will learn which things to say 'No' to; things that are no longer a priority.

Think: Pareto Principle (The 80/20 Rule)

"We know by doing, but we don't always do by knowing."
Anonymous

You've heard of the Pareto Principle. It goes something like this, "80 percent of your sales come from 20 percent of your customers."

It has been applied to all sorts of situations. The numbers aren't always 80/20 but the rule remains. We don't spend enough time on the things that give us the most rewards in life. If you think about it, most of our hard work is going to things that really don't matter in the long-run.

Putting it into Practice

"What is important?" That is a question worth asking yourself. Name the top 5 things that are most important to you? What is the legacy you would like to leave? What is it that you would like your family, friends and colleagues to say about you when you are not in the room? If we don't have a clear idea of what is important, our efforts will easily be diverted. The tendency will be to respond to what we assume is important at the time -- getting pulled in many directions adding to our stress and draining our energy bank.

An over-used strength often becomes a weakness. Be certain that your overdeveloped work habits and underdeveloped emotional support systems are not causing undue stress that can lead to burnout.

Polish Your Work Habits. Be sure that your work habits are not actually causing the very things you hate about your life.

Multitasking Pitfalls

"Time is what we want most, but what we use worst." William Penn

A growing body of scientific research shows one of a woman's favorite time saving techniques, multitasking, can actually make you less efficient. Trying to do two or three things at once or in quick succession can take longer overall than doing them one at a time, and may leave you with reduced brainpower to perform each task.

"When tasks are performed, and especially multiple tasks," David E. Meyer, a mathematical and cognitive psychologist at the University of Michigan, says, "Decisions have to be made by your mind's CEO about which of the resources are going to get used." Driving while using a cellular phone is known to be a dangerous example of multitasking, he adds, because it requires "too many of exactly the same resources, mental and physical." Seconds lost switching between tasks could be the time needed to avoid danger.

Putting it into Practice

Stay focused. Managing two mental tasks at once reduces the brainpower available for either task, according to a study published in the journal *NeuroImage.* Up to 30 percent of U.S. automobile crashes are caused by driver distractions that include mobile communication devices.

Perpetuating the Multitasking Myth. Understand that you can choose to do several things at the same time but know that you are kidding yourself if you think you can do them without cost.   People who multitask are actually less efficient than those who focus on one project at a time, according to a study published in the *Journal of Experimental Psychology*.

Pay very careful attention to how tasks are divided into various subparts. Tasks have natural breakpoints in them, where one part of a task is joined to the next.   If you can manage to stop at these break-points when switching between tasks, that's better than if you stop in midstream while some part of a task is still under way.

The Perils of Multitasking.   If you are engaged in very routine tasks that don't conflict much with each other in terms of their required inputs, outputs and mental processes, then you may be okay.   But when multitasking gets tougher, you are better off to concentrate on just one task at a time. The process of switching back immediately to a task you've just performed, as many multitaskers try to do, takes longer than switching after a bit more time has passed, say findings published by researchers from the *National Institute of Mental Health*. Paul W. Burgess, a neuroscientist at University College, London, says his studies have revealed scant performance differences between male and female multitaskers, though he has found that men and women perceive their multitasking capability differently.

Delegating

"No person will make a great business who wants to do it all himself or get all the credit." Andrew Carnegie

Too many managers fail to delegate appropriately due to the misconception that their abilities are superior to those they manage.

Since attitudes are always reflected in behavior this creates a no-win environment for both you and your staff. This inflated sense of one's own abilities may make you feel good in the short-term but it will ultimately undermine career advancement. Micro-managing continues to be frowned upon by both employees and management.

Delegating is not about relinquishing responsibilities. It is about stretching your people so that they can accomplish tasks in the most efficient and effective manner. Remember, you are accountable for results, not by how much you personally completed.

Putting it into Practice

Their success is your success. Recognize that you ultimately depend on the skills and abilities of your direct reports. We recommend that you jointly work on enhancing the capabilities of each of your team with the use of a condensed Personal Development Plan.

Yes, it takes time. Recognize that this is a front-end investment paying long-term dividends. The sooner your staff becomes more productive, the sooner they will see you as an effective manager - with the ultimate outcome for both- being more satisfied with the job. You are expected to model tolerance and allow staff the freedom to risk and learn.

We all learn from our mistakes. Don't be in too big of a hurry to rush in and rescue a situation, unless it is imperative to do so. All individuals need to be challenged. When they are stuck ask what options they've considered. Experience with hands-on tasks will be their greatest teacher. Once you are a manager, you are expected to teach, mentor and coach.

The Perils of Procrastination

"This is the beginning of a new day. God has given me this day to use as I will. I can waste it or use it for good. What I do today is important, because I am exchanging a day of my life for it. When tomorrow comes, this day will be gone forever, leaving in its place something that I have traded for it. I want it to be gain, not loss; good not evil; success not failure; in order that I shall not regret the price I paid for it." Author Unknown

We all procrastinate. There are simply things we don't like to do, so we put them off. Procrastination becomes a problem when it is creating anxiety or we get negative results.

Many people consider procrastination one of their weaknesses and for good reason. When it becomes an ingrained way of dealing with undesirable tasks, it is viewed by others as a bad habit. There are many reasons for procrastination -- we are too busy; we over estimate or under estimate the amount of work involved; we minimize the negative results when we miss a deadline; we are unsure how to proceed, we allow distractions; we spend too much time thinking about the problem or researching our options, etc. etc.

Putting it into Practice

All big jobs are a series of little jobs. Determine your most productive time of day and start then. Break the task down. Schedule the appropriate amount of time. Focus on one segment at a time. Start doing the most difficult aspect first and give yourself permission to stop when it is done.

Focus and hold yourself accountable. Look at the reason you are procrastinating and recognize that what you are putting off will eventually have to be done. Tomorrow may be the busiest day of the week. Procrastination is costing you in terms of time, energy and your reputation. Remember to under promise and over deliver.

Very few managerial jobs can't be delegated. Before you begin, be sure this is a job that you need to do. Get your ego out of the way. Consider training appropriate staff to take on the tasks you don't enjoy or have time for. Allow them to take credit.

Take Action

"Focus more of your time seeking solutions rather than staying absorbed in the problem." Anonymous

In today's fast paced world, we are always under pressure to make decisions quickly and to move on with the next task at hand.

Gathering more information may be helpful but it can also hold us back. This creates a dilemma – when is it appropriate to obtain more information and when do we move forward with the information we have based on our past experience and knowledge?

Colin Powell gives us some guidelines on when to move forward: Using the formula **P= 40 to 70**, in which **P** stands for probability for success and the numbers indicate the percentage of information required.

Putting it into Practice

Rule of Thumb. Once the information needed is in the 40 to 70 percent range, go with your head, heart and gut. Don't take action if you have only enough information to give you less than a 40 percent chance of being right, but don't wait until you have enough facts to be 100 percent sure, because by then it is almost always too late.

Procrastination steals time. Procrastination is thought to reduce risk but actually increases risk. Excessive delays in the name of information-gathering breeds "analysis paralysis."

Hidden Feelings about the Task. Our assumptions and beliefs based on our past history are always reflected in our decisions and attitudes. It is important to weight the circumstance and identify our emotions about the task. How important is the decision? Are your actions and potential decisions based on reality? Remember, all decisions have an emotional component that may need to be challenged.

Getting Organized

"Don't be fooled by the calendar. There are only as many days in the year as you make use of. One man gets only a week's value out of a year while another man gets a full year's value out of a week." Charles Richards

Our personalities, personal preferences, and our specific strengths require that each of us understand what works best for us in terms of getting organized.

A simplified example is that the linear thinker is content with doing one thing at a time, the visual person will want to be able to see what needs to be done, and the creative type enjoys thinking and doing a number of things all overlapping. To work effectively, we need to understand what works for us. Technology has helped in many ways but it has also overloaded us. We know that if we don't prioritize our activities, we find ourselves spread so thin that we won't have time for those things that are important to us.

Putting it into Practice

Use your calendar efficiently. Whatever system you choose to use, at the beginning of each year go through and highlight all recurring events, whether personal or professional. If preparation is required in advance, i.e. gift buying or your thoughts on annual performance evaluations, note these two weeks prior. Schedule your "Think Times" and also your "Catch-up Times." Use your calendar for follow-ups, tracking projects, or list the names of people to contact, etc.

It all starts with you. Self-management is highly personal but speaks volumes about your ability. Establish your priorities for the week. For each task begin by considering what your desired outcome is. Establish your action steps. Have a 'New Ideas' or 'Opportunities' file on your desktop. File your ideas here so you won't get distracted.

A clean desk shouts an organized individual. Respond to paper in one of four ways: recycle it, write on the top what action you intend to take and put it in your work in progress file; note those things to be filed and put in your out basket, or read it later (save for traveling, or a catch-up day.)

Everyone needs systems. Whatever systems you choose, whatever people you have to assist you, it is important that your systems stay consistent and that everyone is disciplined to follow the routine. Lack of consistency and poor organization habits account for most performance problems.

Get in Alignment with Your To-Do List

"It is not what you know. It is what you are doing with what you know." Peter Urs Bender

Writing things down on a to-do list is a good first step, but it's not enough.

Instead of allowing our minds to perform optimally, many of us fill our brains with daily life's mundane details and rules. Worse, we spend endless hours thinking about the tasks and projects we're trying to juggle.

To cope, we put them on "the list" which often grows faster than we can tick off the tasks. We need a functional system to hold these details until the appropriate time to take action.

Putting it into Practice

Doing what needs to be done. When you add something on your "To Do List" make sure it is something you should be doing.

Don't try to keep multiple to-do lists of undone tasks. When you write down the task yet again, you are blocking your mind from thinking clearly and creatively. The left-brain, that supplies logic and linear thinking, keeps its own list and tends to be untrusting of your multiple to-do lists.

Make sure to prioritize your list. When you complete one task, determine the next priority.

Time Wasters

"Anything that is wasted effort represents wasted time. The best management of our time thus becomes linked inseparable with the best utilization of our efforts." Ted W. Engstom

We all have the same 24 hours in each day. We can either use our time wisely or squander it away. Once the day is gone, it is gone, never to return.

As the saying goes, "The days can feel long but the years are short." Effective managers discipline themselves to use their time intelligently.

Putting it into Practice

Recognize the common ways you fritter away valuable time.
For a two-week period, keep time statistics---recording in 15 minute blocks. Notice where you are frittering away your time. As a start, resist unnecessary interruptions, unscheduled meetings or drop-in visitors especially during your peak performance periods. Discipline yourself around technology. Respond promptly to emails at certain intervals throughout the day. Use call forwarding when you are in a productive mode. You can think of other practices that apply equally to your situation.

Inadequate scheduling. There is a tendency to underestimate the amount of time the most demanding tasks will take. Resist doing the easy jobs first but rather focus on the most important tasks. Schedule more time than you will need in the event you run into the unexpected. This always seems to happen when we are in a time crunch. You know that every big job is a series of little jobs. Delegate the small pieces and see yourself as the coordinator.

Private work time. Some people will choose to work from home, others will arrive at the office well in advance of others, stay late, and still others will work after the children are in bed or commit to allocating some time on weekends. These are catch-up times. They should not become part of the average work week and should be scheduled so you can have no interruptions to provide maximum output. Getting behind, attempting to do too much will send the message that you lack the relevant skills for the job.

Schedule Think Times

"The key is in not spending time, but in investing it." Stephen R. Covey

There are never enough hours in the day. Most business owners or leaders are so busy running their business that they are hard pressed to find the necessary time to think.

For busy people, it feels like the more you do the more that is expected or the more that needs to be done. Time is at a premium. The downside of this dilemma is that oversights are made, significant opportunities are lost, and the organization is spinning its wheels.

An article about Bill Gates, when he was CEO of *Microsoft*, described how he deliberately carved out "Two Think Weeks" a year. During this time, he worked seven days a week, 18 hours a day in self-imposed seclusion to just think. He devoured journals, papers and ideas submitted by employees. By the end of this time, he would have read 100 papers, sent emails to hundreds of people and written a "Think Week" summary for his executives. The results have been impressive.

"The result of one of these ideas led to the development of the Internet browser which sealed Netscape's doom."

Putting it into Practice

Take the time to carve out some dedicated time to think. Reflect on your challenges and opportunities. Instead of two full weeks, you could set aside one or two full days a quarter.

Using unproductive time. Use drive-time, or travel-time to review material that will give you ideas. Don't let the ideas stay dormant. Share them with colleagues and initiate action where you see potential.

Stay creative. Consider using an <u>executive coach</u> to help you brainstorm ideas. Many leaders use a coach for these purposes and schedule one or two hours per month to discuss and clarify their ideas and proposed actions.

Be Clear About Your Availability

"A man only learns in two ways, one by reading, and the other by association with smart people." Will Rogers

Many managers consider it a priority to have an "Open Door Policy" where staff can consult with them at any time of the day on any array of topics.

If the intention is to encourage open communication, feedback and discussion of importance to an employee, then this is a process that also needs to be managed. You need to be responsive to employee needs but you also need to establish time so that you can meet your own deadlines.

Putting it into Practice

Gain control of your time. Establish availability hours – preferably not during your peak performance times.

Limit the time you can spend during these 'Open Door' periods. Listen carefully, ask important questions and if the response requires more than five minutes, s u g g e s t that a meeting or telephone discussion be scheduled.

Establish one-on-one conversations. In addition to ongoing operation discussions, establish routine for one-on-one conversations with all direct reports. These are important meetings since they will keep you informed and create opportunities for open communication. You also need to be kept aware of what has been accomplished and what remains to be done.

Energy, Time and Performance

"Busyness has become a status symbol. If we're busy we must be important." Author Unknown

The lack of energy available within your home and work environment can be the greatest roadblock to managing time well.

Energy predicts your performance outcomes. Just focusing on creating notes and checklists or having well-scheduled calendars or appointments doesn't improve the many demands placed on your time and energy. Too efficient scheduling and control of time can be counterproductive. The efficiency focus creates expectations that clash with the opportunities to develop rich relationships and to enjoy spontaneous moments on a daily basis.

Putting it into Practice

Stop running. Creating a better integration of your work and home life will help you from thinking you are running between priorities.

Building and developing relationships. Opportunities to connect with others in and outside the company can be energizing, as well as productive....since all work results are accomplished through relationships.

Become relational. Rather than focusing on things and time, focus on preserving and enhancing relationships and achieving results.

Your Attitude is Everything

"Ordinary people think merely of spending time. Great people think of using it." Author Unknown

Your attitude is one of the first things people notice about you.

In his book, *"Attitude is Everything,"* Keith Harrell writes, "That you may not be able to change your height or your body type, but you can change your attitude. A positive attitude is not only a product of genetics and heredity but, with proper training, an acquired trait."

Since productive work is all about getting things done with and through others, a negative attitude will cost you dearly in terms of ineffective team work, poorly functioning meetings, and ultimately significant time loss.

Putting it into Practice

Choose an attitude of gratitude. Be recognized as someone who is positive rather than negative. Look to find opportunities where others see problems.

Accept responsibility for your internal dialogue. Recognize and put a stop to the stories we tell ourselves that are not based on fact.

Live your life with purpose and passion. A personal vision will keep you focused and upbeat. Believe in yourself and take on a can-do attitude.

After Thought

Effective time management allows you to be more flexible, not less flexible.

It facilitates you doing the things you really want to do and to become the person you want to be. When you put these newly adopted coaching tips into practice, everything that comes your way becomes organized.

Your systematic decision-making results in clarity, productivity, accountability and empowerment. You easily manage commitments and projects by defining critical objectives and implementation details.

You and your teams do what each of you does best, becoming highly productive while achieving desired outcomes with minimal stress and maximum result.

You reclaim your time and life through better work/life integration.

About the Authors

Barbara A. McEwen is well known as a highly experienced executive, business owner, and seasoned master coach who works with senior executives to help them identify and assess personal development opportunities. Her unique, practical, and powerful strategies make her easy to talk to. She has a way of demystifying what it takes to become more effective. Her coaching deepens the clients' awareness of their unique strengths as a foundation for improvement.

Visit Barb's website at: http://www.2020executivewomen.com

JOHN G. AGNO is a seasoned corporate executive, entrepreneur and management consultant who today coaches senior executives and business owners to reach decision-making clarity by exploring unintended consequences of their future actions.

John helps you see things you are missing, affirms whatever progress you have made, tests your perceptions and lets you know how you are doing. His developmental coaching helps you focus your natural abilities in the right direction.

The coaching allows your inner-potential to erupt upward through effective leadership; to develop commitment within organizations and in a world of "free agents" and "volunteer" talent.

Visit John's websites and blogs for more specific information:

www.CoachedtoSuccess.com

www.SelfAssessmentCenter.com

www.ExecutiveCoaching.us.com

www.CareerWomenCoaching.com

www.BusinessCoaching.us.com

www.LifeSignature.com

www.CoachingTip.com

www.SoBabyBoomer.com

www.Ask-Know-Do.com

For free leadership tips by Coach Agno via email, sign up at:
www.WhatisLeadership.info

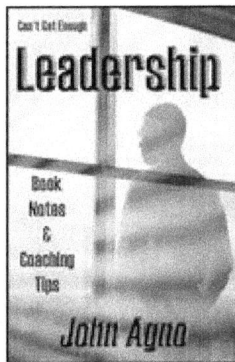

"Can't Get Enough Leadership: Book Notes & Coaching Tips"

By John G. Agno

"**Boomer Retirement Life Tips**" by John G. Agno

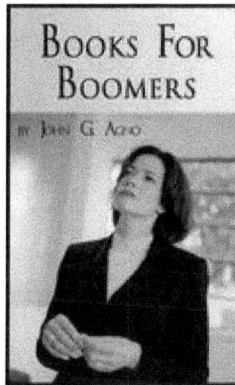

"Books for Boomers: Reviews & Coaching Tips" by John G. Agno

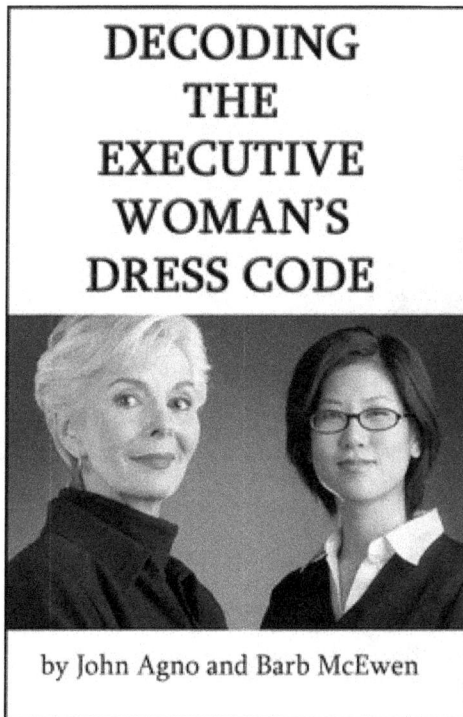

"Decoding the Executive Woman's Dress Code"
By Barb McEwen and John Agno

When Doing It
All Won't Do

A Self-Coaching Guide for Career Women

by

Barb McEwen & John Agno

North America's Top Coaches of Executive Women

"When Doing It All Won't Do: A self–coaching guide for career women" by Barbara McEwen & John G. Agno

www.ingramcontent.com/pod-product-compliance
Lightning Source LLC
Chambersburg PA
CBHW071839020426
42331CB00007B/1789